100 Favorite Kids Meals

by Debbie Madson, Madson Web Publishing, LLC

www.kids-cooking-activities.com

© Copyright

Thanks for reading.

Sign up for a free thank you gift by typing this link into your browser window:

http://www.kids-cooking-activities.com/kids-cooking-activities-newsletter.html

More books in our Menu Planning Series:

100 Kid Favorite Meals

It is hard to title a book Kids Favorite Meals because what is my kids favorite may not be your kids favorite nor is your favorite, my favorite. That is a mouthful, isn't it?!

The important thing is for kids to try new foods, different meals and discover themselves what is their favorite. I know you will find some meals in this book that will become family favorites it may not be all 100 but enough to get your kids eating healthy fun meals.

I encourage you to make your own 100 favorite meals book. It doesn't have to be anything fancy. Type up 100 of your family's favorite meals or place recipe cards in a three-ring binder or recipe file. You don't have 100 recipes? That's okay you really don't need 100 fabulous recipes to feed your family healthy dinners. Start with two weeks' worth or one month's worth or recipes. There is nothing wrong with rotating your recipes week after week.

Just don't forget to occasionally try something new for fun and to discover new interests. Get your kids involved in the planning meals and cooking. Even getting them to rate their meals and give their opinion will get them wanting to try something new. We've included an example of a fun rating sheet/report card on the next page for this purpose.

Find more recipes here:

http://www.kids-cooking-activities.com/kids-recipe-index.html

100 Favorite Meals Table of Contents

Dinner Report Card

It is fun for kids to make dinner into a game. Let kids rate the dinner. Choose your rating and keep track of it on a sheet of paper. You can use a rating like thumbs up, thumbs down. Rate with stars either draw them in the box below or use star stickers for young children. Or you can give dinner a grade A for best- F failed and create the table below into a report card.

However, you choose this is the kids way of trying and rating what they think. This method also helps kids taste new foods so they will be able to rate it.

Dinner	Rating

Pizza Rolls
Ingredients:
Pizza dough store bought or homemade pizza dough recipe
8 ounces mozzarella cheese, cut in cubes
Slices of pepperoni or pepperoni chunks
Ham chunks or ham cut up in small pieces
1/4 cup olive oil
1 teaspoon dried Italian seasoning
3 tablespoons grated Parmesan cheese
2 cups pasta sauce

Directions:
Roll pizza dough onto a floured surface and roll into a large rectangle. For easier handling cut in two batches. Cut into approximately 4-inch squares. On top of each square place a pepperoni and ham slice or chunk and a cheese cube.

Wrap dough around meat, fold sides in and roll up. Press together and fork edges. Place on cookie sheets. In small bowl mix olive oil and seasoning together. With pastry brush, brush oil over pizza bites. Sprinkle with Parmesan cheese. Use all dough and bake at 400 degrees for 15-18 minutes. Use pasta sauce for dipping.

How to Make Sloppy Joes

This is one of my favorite recipes and a family favorite. It is a recipe that is loaded with lots of vegetables. The pureed vegetables really add a lot of flavor to this sloppy joe recipe. It also freezes well.

You can use ground hamburger, ground chicken or a mixture of both. I usually use 1 pound of each and then I have extra to freeze for another meal.

Ingredients:

2 lbs. ground hamburger, ground chicken or combination
1 large onion, chopped
3 carrots, chopped
2 celery stalks, chopped
1 green pepper, chopped
1 Tablespoon vinegar
1 cup catsup
1 Tablespoons Worcestershire sauce
1 Tablespoons mustard

Directions:

In blender add onion, carrots, celery and green pepper. Continue to add vinegar, catsup, Worcestershire sauce and mustard in blender. Puree. Add to large skillet and cook with ground hamburger. Break up and stir meat. Simmer cooking about 10-15 minutes.

Taco Chili

Ingredients:

16 oz. kidney beans

2 Tablespoons or more to taste, taco seasoning mix

2-16 oz. can tomatoes

1 lb. Ground beef cooked

1 1/2 Cups water

Directions:

Mix soup ingredients together and cook in the crock pot or on the stove for 30 minutes or less. Serve with toppings below.

Toppings:

small avocado, diced

cheddar cheese, shredded

sour cream

tortilla chips

*I often puree any vegetables I have on hand like zucchini or carrots and add it to the soup. It thickens the soup as well as adds more flavor and nutrition.

Lemon Teriyaki Chicken

Ingredients:

½ Cup lemon juice

½ Cup soy sauce

¼ Cup sugar

3 Tablespoons brown sugar

2 Tablespoons water

2 garlic cloves chopped

½ teaspoon ginger

6 chicken breasts, chicken thighs or drumsticks

Directions:

Add all ingredients together in Ziploc bag except chicken. Blend together. Add chicken and freeze. When ready to cook, pour everything into a casserole dish and bake or add to skillet and cook over medium.

Stuffed Bell Peppers Recipe

This stuffed bell peppers recipe is great for hiding a few extra vegetables in the rice and hamburger mixture.

Ingredients:
6 bell peppers
1 onion
1 carrot
1 chicken bouillon cube
2 cups cooked rice
1 lb. ground beef
1/2 cup tomato sauce

Directions:
Preheat oven to 350 degrees. Bring a pan of water to boil and place peppers cut in half lengthwise or whole with tops cut off and seeds removed. Boil several minutes. Drain and set aside. Add 1-2 tablespoons oil to a frying pan. Grate 1 onion and 1 peeled carrot into oil. Sauté 1 minute.

Add 2 cups rice and 1 bouillon cube. Stir several minutes until rice turns glassy. Stir in 2 cups water. Turn to medium low and simmer with a lid on. Meanwhile in separate bowl, add 1 lb. uncooked ground beef and 1/2 cup tomato sauce together. Add in rice and stir to combine. Stuff peppers and bake at 350 degrees for 30-35 minutes.

You can add even more nutrition and vegetables by adding pureed vegetables to your hamburger mixture. This way if kids don't like or eat all the bell pepper itself they are still getting lots of nutrition in the meat rice mix.

Hawaiian Haystacks

This Hawaiian Haystacks recipe is a fun kids' meal where everyone can create their own rice haystack with sauce and toppings. It gets its Hawaiian name for the tropical fruit you add to the top and because you pile the toppings on like a haystack.

<u>First prepare the sauce</u>
1 can cream chicken soup
¼ Cup water, chicken broth or milk *
Cooked chicken pieces as much as desired

Directions:
Stir all ingredients together in a saucepan. Heat on medium-low.
*If you would like a thicker sauce, add less liquid to make a thinner sauce add more liquid.

Have the following ingredients available as you desire and let everyone assemble their haystacks.

- Cooked rice
- Sauce
- Vegetable ideas: chopped tomatoes, celery, green peppers, onions, mushrooms, whatever you'd like or have available.
- Fruit ideas: chopped pineapple, sliced bananas, mandarin oranges
- Shredded cheddar cheese
- Slivered almonds
- Shredded coconut
- Chow Mein noodles

Let each family member add cooked rice to their bowl, shredded cheese then sauce. Top with vegetables, fruits and toppings of your choice. These are fun for kids as they get to pick and choose their toppings. Encourage them to add some vegetables and fruit to their haystack as well. (Even if it is on the side of the haystack.)

Homemade Pizza Dough

You will see with these homemade pizza dough recipes, making fresh pizza at home can be delicious and easier than you think.

Pizza Dough

Ingredients:
2 ½ Cups flour
1 teaspoon Salt
1 Cup warm water
1 Tablespoon yeast
1 Tablespoon Italian seasoning, optional
1 Tablespoon oil

Directions:
Dissolve yeast in warm water and add a dash of sugar. Meanwhile, in mixing bowl add flour, salt, oil and Italian seasoning. When yeast is bubbly and ready pour into flour mixture and blend. Form into a ball and place in an oiled bowl. Let rise 30-60 minutes. Prepare pizza toppings and place in bowls on table.

~You can substitute white flour for wheat flour or half and half in these recipes. The important thing to remember is to start your pizza dough 1 -1 1/2 hour before you are ready to eat. Letting your dough sit for 1 hour will result in a much more airy and delicious crust.

Pizza Topping Ideas:

Spaghetti sauce, Mozzarella cheese, shredded, pepperoni slices
Ham slices or Canadian bacon, Pineapple chunks, Pepper slices
Sliced mushrooms, Sliced olives, chopped fresh broccoli

If you don't have time or want to make one of these homemade pizza crust recipes, try these options for pizza crusts.

Quick Pizza Crust Ideas

English muffins, split in half, Bagels, split in half, French Bread, cut in half lengthwise, Pita bread, Readymade crust, Tortillas

Recipe for Making Tacos

Arrange your taco toppings around the table and prepare your meat. The family can assemble their own tacos.

Taco Toppings

Shredded cheese, Shredded lettuce, Sliced olives, Chopped onions, Salsa, Sour cream, Guacamole

Simple Ground Beef Taco Recipe

1 lb. hamburger
Taco seasoning mix
1/4 Cup water
Directions:
Brown hamburger and drain. Add in seasoning and 1/4 cup water. Let simmer 5 minutes.

Ground Beef Taco Recipe with Beans

1 lb. hamburger
1 can refried beans
1/4 cup water
2-3 Tablespoons taco seasoning mix
Directions:
Brown hamburger and drain off grease. Stir in refried beans and water. Stir in taco seasoning mix and heat several minutes.

Simple Chicken Taco Recipe

Shredded cooked chicken (leftover chicken or a rotisserie chicken meat)
Salsa
Kidney beans or black beans
Shredded cheese
Directions:
Stir salsa into shredded chicken. Use as much salsa as your family likes. To assemble your tacos top tortillas with chicken, beans and cheese.

Beef and Bean Enchiladas

These can be prepared the night before or in the morning and placed in the fridge until dinner time. You can also make extra and freeze for another night.

Ingredients:
1 can refried beans (*see note below)
Ground hamburger
2 cups cooked rice
1 medium onion
Shredded cheddar cheese
Whole wheat tortillas
Salsa
~Serve with sour cream, salsa or guacamole

Directions:
Grate one medium onion with a cheese grater into a skillet. Add hamburger and brown until no longer pink. Drain and stir in refried beans and cooked rice until well combined. Place a large spoonful on a tortilla and roll up. Sprinkle with cheese.

Place seam side down in a casserole dish. Continue with remaining mixture and spread salsa on the top. Sprinkle tortillas with cheese. Bake at 350 degrees for 20 minutes.

*You can change the beans around by using kidney beans, chili beans, white beans or black beans in place of the refried beans. Or for more nutrition and super delicious try a variety of two beans such as refried beans and black beans.

Stroganoff

Our family loves this basic beef stroganoff and I really love it becau
easy and tastes delicious. Boil water for noodles while you are cooking the
stroganoff.

Ingredients:
1 lb. steak, cut in small chunks
1/4 cup flour
1- 8 oz. tomato sauce
1 8 oz. can sliced mushrooms
1 Cup beef broth or 2 beef bouillon cubes dissolved in 1 Cup water
8 oz. or less as desired, sour cream

Directions:
In a bowl, toss steak and 1/4 cup flour until well coated. Brown in oil in a
skillet. Add 1-2 Tablespoons tomato sauce and add mushrooms. Cook
several minutes. Add beef broth and heat until bubbly. Allow to cook 5-10
minutes until sauce thickens. Add sour cream. Serve with warm egg noodles
or rice.

Kung Pao Chicken

This kung pao chicken recipe is delicious. Once you break it down into steps you will see it doesn't take as much work as you might think.

Ingredients:
1 lb. Chicken breasts, cubed
1 teaspoon cornstarch
¼ Cup water
¼ Cup soy sauce
4 teaspoons cornstarch
1 Tablespoon sugar
1 teaspoon vinegar
4-5 dashes of hot pepper sauce
Garlic clove
3-4 green onions
1-2 green peppers
1 Cup peanuts, optional

Directions:
Cut 1 lb. boneless chicken breasts into cubes. In bowl, stir together chicken and 1 teaspoon cornstarch. Set aside.

Prepare sauce by combining the following ingredients: 1/4 Cup water, 1/4 Cup soy sauce, 4 teaspoons cornstarch, 1 Tablespoon sugar, 1 teaspoon vinegar, 4-5 dashes of hot pepper sauce. Set aside.

Prepare vegetables. 1 clove of garlic, minced 3-4 green onions, sliced 1-2 green peppers, chopped.

Lightly brown 1 Cup peanuts in oil. Set aside. In same pan, sauté garlic, green onions and green peppers in oil. Set aside. In same pan, fry chicken in oil until brown and done. Combine vegetables, peanuts and chicken together in pan and add sauce. Cook several minutes. Serve with hot rice.

Chicken Broccoli Casserole

Feel free to substitute any vegetable you'd like in this recipe.

Ingredients:
4 chicken breasts (or one for each person)
can cream mushroom or chicken soup (or see homemade recipe below6)
1 cup milk
small package of broccoli
1 Cup cheddar cheese, shredded
Pepper, and paprika to taste
bread crumbs or crushed cornflakes

Directions:
In casserole dish, lay chicken breasts on bottom of pan. Add broccoli on top of chicken. In a medium bowl, add mushroom soup and milk. Stir until well blended. Season with pepper and paprika but no salt. The mushroom soup will have salt in it already. Spread mushroom soup over top of chicken. Bake for 35-40 minutes at 375 degrees. Top with cheddar cheese and bread crumbs and bake until cheese is melted.

Homemade Cream of Chicken Soup
Ingredients:
1/3 cup butter or stick margarine
1/3 cup all-purpose flour
1/4 teaspoon pepper
1 3/4 cups chicken broth
2/3 cup milk

Directions:
In saucepan melt butter. Whisk in flour until thickens. Whisk in chicken broth and pepper. Bring to a boil until thickens. Whisk in milk and again bring to a boil until thickens set aside and allow to cool.

Homemade Potato Casserole

You can prepare this ahead of time even overnight and cook when ready. You can stir in chopped ham in the casserole too.

Prepare cream soup below first and allow to cool.

Homemade Cream Chicken Soup

Ingredients:

1/3 cup butter or stick margarine

1/3 cup all-purpose flour

1/4 teaspoon pepper

1 3/4 cups chicken broth

2/3 cup milk

Directions:

In saucepan melt butter. Whisk in flour until thickens. Whisk in chicken broth and pepper. Bring to a boil until thickens. Whisk in milk and again bring to a boil until thickens set aside and allow to cool.

To prepare potato casserole

Ingredients:

¼ Cup onions

2 Tablespoons butter

5-6 medium potatoes

1/2-1 Cup shredded cheese

Cream chicken soup, recipe above

Directions:

Sauté 1/4 cup onions in 2 Tablespoons butter. Season with salt and pepper. Peel 5-6 medium potatoes and dice. Add potatoes to casserole dish. Season with salt and pepper.

Stir in sautéed onions. Sprinkle with 1/2-1 Cup shredded cheese.
Pour cream chicken sauce over top. Cook at 350 degrees for 40 minutes or until tender.

Lettuce Wraps

Ingredients:

3 Tablespoons soy sauce
3 Tablespoons honey
1 Tablespoon ginger, fresh
1 tsp fresh garlic
4 chicken breasts, chopped in small pieces
2 carrots, diced
lettuce leaves

Directions:

Cook chicken and carrots in skillet until no longer pink. Meanwhile, blend together soy sauce, honey ginger and garlic. Pour sauce into chicken and allow to cook several minutes.

Wash and dry lettuce leaves. Add 1/4 Cup or more chicken carrot mixture into a lettuce leave and roll up. Serve immediately.

Chicken or Turkey Stuffing Casserole

You can make a turkey casserole recipe easily by substituting turkey for chicken in any of your favorite recipes. Here is one of our favorite's using stuffing and turkey. This recipe is great using Thanksgiving leftovers or any time of year you are craving Thanksgiving.

Ingredients:

Box of stuffing mix, cooked
Turkey, chopped or shredded
Thin noodles, cooked
1 can each of cream mushroom soup, cream celery, cream chicken soup
bag of frozen peas and carrots mix
Milk

Directions:

Place stuffing mix on bottom of pan. Place turkey pieces on top. Add in peas and carrots mix. Add cooked noodles and can cream soups. Add 1 1/2 cans of milk. Bake at 350 for 1 hour.

Recipe for Chicken Parmesan

My kids love this recipe for Chicken Parmesan. It is easy to make and can be prepared ahead of time by doing all the prep work and cooking at dinner time.

Ingredients:
1 egg
1/4 Cup bread crumbs
1/4 Cup Parmesan cheese
4-6 chicken breasts
small jar spaghetti sauce
1 Cup mozzarella cheese
pasta noodles

Directions:
Spray a casserole dish and set aside. Lay two separate dishes or pie plates next to each other. Add egg in one and beat. In another dish, add bread crumbs and Parmesan cheese. Dip each chicken breast in egg and then coat with bread crumbs.

(You can use egg, buttermilk or milk to soak your chicken in.)

Place in casserole dish. Pour spaghetti sauce over chicken and sprinkle with mozzarella cheese. Use as much sauce as you would like. Bake 400 degrees for 15-20 minutes.

While your chicken is cooking cook any size of noodles you'd like to serve with the chicken parmesan and serve with extra spaghetti sauce.

Kids can help coat chicken just make sure they wash their hands well after handling chicken. They can also help prepare a fruit salad or green salad to go with dinner.

Deep Dish Pizza Crust Recipe

Ingredients:
3 Cups flour
2 Tablespoons oil
2 eggs
1 Cup warm water
1 teaspoon salt
1 Tablespoon yeast
pinch of sugar

Directions:
In a measuring cup add warm water, yeast and pinch of sugar. Set aside. In a mixing bowl add flour, salt, oil and eggs. Blend together. Pour water mixture in your dough and allow to mix several minutes. Take out and knead several minutes. Let set for 1 hour.

Pat dough in 2- 8 or 9-inch circle pans and press up the edges. Add your sauce, cheese and pizza toppings. Bake at 425 degrees for 30-35 minutes until golden brown.

Cordon Bleu Casserole

Ingredients:

2-3 cups chicken chopped

2 cups cubed ham

1-2 Cups small pasta shells, cooked

1 cup cubed cheddar cheese

Cream of chicken soup

1/2-1 cup sour cream

1/2-1 cup milk

Directions:

Cook pasta shells and drain. Cook chicken and place in a casserole dish. Layer ham, cooked pasta shells and cubed cheese on top of chicken. In a mixing bowl, stir together cream of chicken soup, sour cream and milk. Blend together and stir in ham and chicken mixture. Bake at 350 degrees for 20-25 minutes.

...tti or Lasagna

...asy manicotti recipe can be changed and used for other noodles such ...asagna or stuffed shells. The addition of frozen spinach makes this a great spinach manicotti recipe but it can be left out if desired.

Ingredients:
1 box manicotti noodles
1 cup mozzarella cheese, shredded
2 Cups cottage cheese
¾ Cup grated parmesan cheese
2 Tablespoons parsley
1 egg, beaten
pinch of salt and pepper
1/2-1 cup frozen chopped spinach, thawed
jar of spaghetti sauce

Directions:
Bring a pot of water to boil and add a pinch of salt. Cook noodles and prepare cheese mixture. Squeeze the excess water out of your thawed spinach. Add to mixing bowl. Continue to add mozzarella, cottage and parmesan cheese. Stir in parsley, egg, spinach and season with salt and pepper. Stir together to combine.

When noodles are cooked, allow to cool slightly so you can handle them. In a casserole dish, pour a small amount of spaghetti sauce on bottom of pan just to cover. With small spoon or hands add cheese mixture into noodles. Line in casserole dish. Continue to fill noodles.
Top with spaghetti sauce and more mozzarella cheese, if desired. Bake at 350 degrees for 35-40 minutes.
~If you are using large shells follow recipe as above stuffing shells instead.

Easy Lasagna Recipe

Want to know how to make lasagna with this recipe? It is super easy to create an easy lasagna using this same recipe. Cook your noodles and prepare cheese mixture as described above. Pour small bit of spaghetti sauce on bottom of pan. Layer noodles, cheese mixture and spaghetti sauce. Continue making layers until mixture is gone. Bake 350 degrees for 35-40 minutes.

Homemade Spaghetti Sauce

Sure, you can open a jar of spaghetti sauce but this is so much better and has no preservatives in it that it is worth the extra effort. You can also add puree vegetables to the sauce to boost the nutrition.

Ingredients:
2 Tablespoons olive oil
1 onion, chopped
1 garlic clove, crushed
1 teaspoon Italian seasoning
1/4 teaspoon cayenne pepper
1 lb. Beef
28 oz + small can of tomatoes equals 5 Cup chopped tomatoes and run through blender
1/2 Cup ketchup
2 Tablespoons Worcestershire sauce
2 tsp. dried oregano
salt and pepper

Directions:
Heat oil in pan and sauté onion and garlic. Stir in herbs and cayenne. Add beef and cook until browned. Stir in tomatoes, ketchup, tomato paste, Worcestershire sauce, oregano and pepper. Pour in stock and bring to boil. Cover and lower heat simmer for at least 30 minutes or place in crock pot and cook 6-8 hours on low.

Manti with Yogurt Sauce

My husband spent some time in Turkey and loved the ravioli with yogurt sauce. We reinvented it a little and it is one of our favorites. My kids often eat it without the sauce. For special occasions, we make fresh ravioli with pork inside and top it with this sauce.

Meat filled ravioli -homemade, frozen or fresh

Sauce Ingredients:

1 Cup plain yogurt

pinch of salt

1 teaspoon Parsley

3 cloves of garlic, minced

2 Tablespoons Melted butter

Directions:

Boil 8 quarts water. Gently add pasta to boiling water and simmer under reduced heat for 5 minutes or until ravioli rise to the top. Taste pasta for doneness. Mix sauce ingredients together and pour over cooked pasta squares. Serve immediately.

Garlic Sauce Pasta

This starts with making a roux or a white sauce. The secret with this recipe is to serve it immediately. Once you mix your noodles with the sauce it is best right then don't let it sit and then eat it! If you need to prepare ahead, leave the sauce separated from the noodles until right before serving.

Ingredients:

2 Tablespoons butter
2 cloves garlic
2 Tablespoons flour
3/4 Cup chicken broth
3/4 Cup milk
2 teaspoons parsley
pinch of salt and pepper
1/3 Cup parmesan cheese
8 oz. noodles, any shape or size

Directions:

Start boiling water to cook your noodles. Meanwhile prepare sauce and add noodles to boiling water when ready. Sauté garlic in butter. Whisk flour into butter and blend until smooth. Mixture will thicken slightly. Slowly whisk in chicken broth. Allow to heat slightly.

Blend in milk and parsley. Add a dash of salt and pepper. Stir in cheese and allow to melt. Allow to cook several minutes on low while waiting for noodles to finish cooking. Drain noodles and pour sauce over top. Serve immediately. You can also stir in cooked vegetables such as broccoli or peas.

Chopped cooked chicken can be added to the noodles before serving also.

Barbecue Pork Chops

You can prepare these barbecued pork chops in the crock pot such as the directions say below or in the oven for 45 minutes-1 hour or until tender.

Ingredients:
1/2 Cup water
2 Tablespoons sugar
1 teaspoon salt
1/4 Cup vinegar
1 Tablespoon mustard
1/2 teaspoon pepper
1/2 Cup ketchup
2 Tablespoons Worcestershire sauce

Directions:
Add all ingredients in a large measuring cup and whisk together.

Add pork chops to crock pot and pour barbecue sauce over the top. Cook on low 6 hours. You can use this same barbecue recipe with chicken or roast and prepare in the crock pot same as above.

Peachy Pork Chops

Ingredients:

can cream mushroom soup

1 Tablespoon Worcestershire sauce

¼ Cup water

½ teaspoon cinnamon

peach juice from 8 oz. can peaches

6 boneless pork chops

2 Cups fresh peaches or canned peaches

Directions:

Combine cinnamon, soup, Worcestershire sauce, peach juice and water in bowl. Stir together. Place pork chops in crock pot and pour mixture over top. Place peaches over pork chops. Cook 4-6 hours.

Meatball Soup
Ingredients:
6 oz. ground turkey
large beaten egg
3 tablespoons bread crumbs
parsley
1 teaspoon salt
¼ teaspoon pepper
6 Cups chicken broth
2 medium carrots, peeled and sliced
1 potato peeled and chopped
1 Cup pasta bowtie, optional
chopped parsley, optional

Directions:
Combine turkey, egg, bread crumbs and parsley and form into meatballs. In saucepan cook broth and add carrots. Bring to a boil and add pasta cook 5 minutes. Lower heat and add meatballs. Simmer until cooked through.

Easy Hamburger Soup

Ingredients:
1 large can tomato juice
2 cups water
8 oz. elbow macaroni or alphabet pasta, cooked
1 lb. ground hamburger
salt and pepper

Directions:
Cook noodles and drain. Meanwhile, cook ground hamburger. Combine macaroni, cooked hamburger, tomato juice, water and pepper to taste.
If you are preparing this recipe ahead of time, leave the pasta separate from the soup. When it is dinner time warm up the soup and add pasta and soup together right before serving. The pasta noodles will soak up the juice otherwise.

8 Layer Salad Recipe
Ingredients:
1 Cup noodles, cooked
3 Cups shredded lettuce
3-4 hard cooked eggs, sliced
salt and pepper
1 Cup chopped cooked ham
1 Cup chopped salami
1 pkg. Frozen peas, thawed
½ Cup mayonnaise
¼ Cup sour cream
1 teaspoon mustard
1 Cup cheese

Directions:
Cook macaroni and rinse with cold water. In serving bowl, (I like to use a glass bowl so you can see the layers) place lettuce on bottom, top with cooked noodles, cooked chopped eggs, chopped ham, salami and peas.

Combine mayo, sour cream and mustard together and spread over the top. Refrigerate overnight. Sprinkle with cheese before serving.

Cooking Tips

This needs to be prepared ahead of time and overnight is even better. Cook the macaroni and eggs at the same time while you are shredding lettuce, chopping ham and salami. Kids are great at washing and shredding lettuce. They can add in the ingredients in the correct layer.

Individual Layer Salad Recipe
Another fun way to serve this is in small individual glass or plastic cups that everyone can have their own layer salad. If they don't like the salad dressing leave it off or use a type they do like.

Chicken or Pork Fried Rice

Add or subtract any vegetables you choose or use chicken or shrimp in place of pork.

Ingredients:
3 cups cooked rice
Pork cut in small cubes
Oil for frying pork
chopped carrots, chopped bell peppers
Fresh or frozen peas, thawed
2 eggs
3 Tablespoons soy sauce

Directions:
In skillet, cook pork in 1 tablespoon oil until no longer pink. Add in rice, shredded carrots. Cook and stir about 5-8 minutes until warmed through. Push rice along sides making a crater in the middle. Break 2 eggs in crater and cook and stir until scrambled. When eggs are completely cooked stir eggs into the rice mixture and add peas and soy sauce.

Egg Drop Soup

A great recipe for egg drop soup. Super easy, healthy and kid friendly. It goes great with the fried rice.

Ingredients:

6 Cups chicken broth

3 eggs, beaten

1 Tablespoon soy sauce

green onions, chopped for topping, optional

green peas, optional

Directions:

In soup pan add chicken broth and soy sauce. In a cup, beat 3 eggs. In your cup add a ladle full of soup and beat together. Slowly stir eggs into boiling soup. If desired add in peas and onions. Serve immediately.

Simple Taco Salad
Ingredients:
Ground hamburger or chicken cubes
Taco seasoning
Kidney beans
Shredded cheddar cheese
Shredded lettuce
Chopped tomatoes
Sliced olives

Directions:
Cook hamburger or chicken and season with taco seasoning and pepper.
Have kids shred lettuce and mix salad ingredients together.

~Another way you can serve this is in individual bowls and everyone in the family can build their own taco salad.

Beef Stew
Ingredients:
1-2 lbs. Beef stew meat, cubed
salt and pepper
In a large measuring cup or bowl stir together:
6-8 Cups beef broth
1 teaspoon Worcestershire sauce
1 clove garlic
½ teaspoon Paprika
2 teaspoon seasoned salt
2 teaspoons brown sugar
Set aside and chop vegetables below.
3 carrots, sliced
3 potatoes, diced
1 onion chopped
1 stalk celery

Directions:
Place meat in large Ziploc bag. Season with salt and pepper. Pour beef broth mixture over the top. Add chopped carrots, onion, celery and potatoes to bag. Seal and freeze. When ready to cook allow to unthaw overnight and pour into crock pot cook on high 8 hours.

Tin Foil Dinners

For tin foil dinners, you can use whatever meat you choose, chicken breast, pork chops or beef cubes all work well. Our favorite is a hamburger patty and that is what is included in the recipe below, feel free to change it if you'd like. You can also add more or different vegetables as you would like. Kids love to prepare their own packet dinner themselves so have all the ingredients out and let them assemble their own.

Ingredients:
Hamburger patty -one for each person
Carrot sticks or circles
Potatoes, cut in circles or small chunks 1-2 per person depending on size
Frozen green beans
Onion, cut in rings
Cream of mushroom soup or homemade version
Seasoning salt
Dry onion soup mix, optional

Directions:
Tear off large sheet of tin foil, one for each person. Shape hamburger into patties. Prepare carrots, potatoes, and onion by cutting into circles or small chunks. Arrange everything on kitchen counter and let family assemble their own dinner. Start with the hamburger (or other meat) on the bottom. Season with seasoning salt. Top with vegetables. Sprinkle with more salt and a shake of dry onion soup mix. Add one or two spoonfuls of cream of mushroom soup. This will help make a gravy. Wrap up tin foil. If needed use another sheet of tin foil to make secure. Write name on each packet hamburger foil dinner. Place on a cookie sheet in case the tin foil dinner leaks juice. Bake at 350 degrees for 30 minutes. Check one tin foil packet to see if meat is cooked through and potatoes are tender. Be careful of steam when opening dinners.

Ham and Vegetable Soup

Change your vegetables around in this Ham Vegetable Soup recipe if you'd like. Sometimes I've added chopped carrots and celery instead of potatoes or along with them.

Ingredients:

8 Cup chicken broth
2 medium potatoes, cubed or equal to 2 Cups cubed
1 ½ Cup broccoli flowerets and 1 Cup cauliflower flowerets or use small bag of broccoli/cauliflower mix
¼ teaspoon nutmeg, optional
cubed ham as much as you'd like

Directions:

Combine broth and potatoes in a saucepan and bring to a boil. Reduce heat and simmer until potatoes are tender. Stir in broccoli, cauliflower and nutmeg. Simmer 5 minutes until vegetables are tender. Stir in chopped ham and heat through. **Serve with breadsticks use recipe below if desired.

Meatloaf

rumbled

crackers crushed
5 Tablespoons shredded Swiss cheese
4 ½ teaspoons chopped onion
1 garlic clove, minced
¼ teaspoon salt
1/8 teaspoon pepper
½ lb. Ground beef

Directions:
In bowl combine egg, crackers, 4 Tablespoons shredded cheese, chopped onion, garlic, bacon, salt and pepper. Add beef into mixture and combine. Shape into loaf and freeze wrapped in tin foil or in a Ziploc bag. When ready to cook take out of the freezer and place in a loaf pan. Top with more bacon pieces if desired. Bake at 350 degrees for 30 minutes- 1 hour. Test with a meat thermometer.

Chicken Quiche

Ingredients:
2-3 Cups Chicken, shredded
1 1/2 Cups milk
3 eggs
1 1/2 Cups shredded cheese
*optional, 1/2 package frozen chopped broccoli thawed

Directions:
In a bowl add shredded chicken to milk, eggs, and shredded cheese. Season with salt and pepper. Blend together and pour into a pie crust. Bake for 40 minutes at 375 degrees or until lightly browned and knife inserted in middle comes out clean.

Calzone Dough Recipe

You can make a variety of fillings to go with this calzone dough recipe. These freeze well so it is a great idea to make a large batch for another night.

Calzone Dough
Ingredients:
2 ½ Cups flour

1 teaspoon Salt

1 Cup warm water

1 Tablespoon yeast

1 Tablespoon Italian seasoning, opt.

1 Tablespoon oil

Directions:
Dissolve yeast in warm water and add a dash of sugar. Meanwhile, in mixing bowl add flour, salt, oil and Italian seasoning. When yeast is bubbly and ready pour into flour mixture and blend. Form into a ball and place in an oiled bowl. Let rise 30-60 minutes. Separate dough into desired number of calzones. Roll each ball of dough into a circle. Prepare your calzone dough and follow directions above. Top half of each calzone circle with desired toppings. Fold over dough and roll edges together. Pinch seams together.
In a large measuring cup add oil, basil and Parmesan cheese together. Whisk until blended. With a pastry brush, brush the top of each calzone. Bake at 450 degrees for 10-15 minutes.

Ham and Cheese Calzone
2 cups diced fully cooked ham or sliced pepperoni

2 cups mozzarella cheese, shredded

Parmesan cheese, optional

Dried basil, optional

Top calzone with ham and cheese and sprinkle with parmesan and basil. You can also substitute cheddar cheese for the mozzarella.

Cream of Potato Soup

Ingredients:

2 Cups potatoes, cubed
1 small onion, optional
1 carrot
1 celery stalk
1 cup cauliflower pieces
Water to cover
2 teaspoons chicken bouillon or 2 cubes
1/4 Cup milk

Directions:

Cut vegetables into slices or cubes. In soup pan place potatoes, onion, carrot, celery and cauliflower. Add water to cover up vegetables. Cook and simmer on medium until vegetables are tender. Add half of soup mixture into blender. Add bouillon and milk to blender also. Puree several seconds. Add back to saucepan and stir together. Allow to cool and freeze in smaller containers.

Jambalaya

Ingredients:
1 package polish kielbasa or sausage, whatever your family likes
1 1/2 cups uncooked white rice
1 1/2 cups chicken broth
1/4 tsp dried thyme
1/4 teaspoon chili powder
Green pepper or other color, chopped
One carrot, grated
1 small onion, quartered
1 can chopped tomatoes, undrained

Directions:
Cut sausage into slices. In large skillet, cook sausage flipping over and browning each side. Set aside and wipe out grease from pan. Add uncooked rice, chicken broth, thyme, chili powder, chopped pepper, grated carrot, quartered onion and chopped tomatoes with juice to your skillet. Stir all together and add sausage back to the pan. Cover with a lid and simmer on medium about 10-15 minutes until rice is done.

If you are using brown rice keep in mind the cooking time will be different as brown rice takes much longer than white rice. If you'd like you can also add shrimp before simmering.

Barbecue Roast Beef

This beef roast is easiest prepared in a crock pot and cooked for 6-8 hours but you can also cook it in the oven for one hour depending on the size of your roast. Add cut potatoes, onions, turnips or carrots with your roast and you have dinner ready all in one pot.

Ingredients:
beef (or substitute a pork roast)
1-2 onions, chopped
1/2 Cup water
salt and pepper

Directions:

Place meat, onions and water in crock pot. Season with salt and pepper. Cook 6-8 hours. Drain and set broth aside for later. Let sit for 5-10 minutes then cut or shred. If you are preparing roast beef in the oven, place roast in a large casserole pan and bake for 40 minutes-1 hour depending on how big your roast is. Bake at 350 degrees. If you are adding vegetables place inside the crock pot and season with salt and pepper also. You can also add vegetables to your roast in the oven. Just place vegetables along the sides of your pan. You can reserve the broth after your roast beef is done cooking, to make gravy, barbecue sauce recipe below or discard.

Barbecue Sauce
Ingredients:
1/2 Cup meat broth (broth you drained and set aside from above)
1 Cups ketchup
1 teaspoon mustard
1 Tablespoons vinegar
1 1/2 Tablespoons brown sugar
1 1/2 Tablespoons Worcestershire sauce
Salt and pepper to taste

Directions:

Combine all sauce ingredients in a measuring cup. Stir shredded meat into the sauce and pour back in the crock pot for about 20 minutes or warm in the microwave or oven. Serve shredded meat on buns or rolls. Or serve the sauce on the side with the meat for dipping.

Hamburger Noodle Casserole

My kids and I love this creamy hamburger noodle casserole. It tastes like lasagna in a casserole but with a few different ingredients. I usually prepare this the night before and leave it in the fridge. It also is a great kid friendly recipe to take to a potluck dinner or when company comes over.

Ingredients:

8 ounces cream cheese

8 ounces sour cream

1 cup cottage cheese

1 lb. lean ground beef

Jar of spaghetti sauce

Pasta noodles, whatever shape you'd like

Mozzarella cheese, shredded

Directions:

Cook noodles. Meanwhile, in mixing bowl combine cream cheese, sour cream and cottage cheese. Drain noodles when done cooking and stir into cheese mixture. Set aside. Brown hamburger in a skillet and drain well. Mix in spaghetti sauce. In a casserole dish, spread spaghetti sauce on bottom. Layer with noodle mixture and top with more spaghetti sauce. Sprinkle with mozzarella cheese and bake at 350 degrees for 20-25 minutes.

Homemade Salad Bar Night

Serve with breadsticks. In separate dishes add all ingredients you'd like to use lined out like a buffet.

I use any of the following I have on hand.

Ingredients:
Lettuce
Fresh spinach
Chopped vegetables:
(our favorites are carrots, cucumbers, tomatoes, broccoli, cauliflower)
hard boiled eggs sliced
sliced or whole olives
chopped ham or turkey
chopped cooked chicken
Shredded cheese
Salad dressings
sunflower seeds
bacon bits
croutons

Ham and Cheese Quiche

Ingredients:
Pie dough
6 eggs
1/2 Cup milk
Shredded cheese
Chopped ham
One of the following vegetables, such as shredded carrots, shredded zucchini or cooked chopped broccoli, optional

Directions:
In a bowl, add eggs, milk, cheese and ham. Adding as much cheese and ham as desired. Stir until well blended. Add in vegetables if you choose. Using a large glass cut pie dough into small circles to fit into a muffin cup. Place a circle of pie dough into each muffin hole. Pour egg mixture into each hole. Bake at 375 degrees for about 25 minutes or until knife inserted in center comes out clean. Serve with chopped tomatoes, salsa or hot sauce. Add a fruit salad that kids can help prepare.

Sandwich Night

Okay, so some nights are just the perfect nights for a sandwich bar type dinner. We usually have a variety of choices including:

Deli meat

Tuna fish

Chicken salad

Ham salad

Egg salad

BLT

I usually have 2-3 choices depending on what I have on hand. No matter what the meal is kids like to be able to choose what they have. You can vary what your sandwich is made from also such as a bagel, mini rolls, sandwich bread, croissant, tortilla, etc. I serve a vegetable platter on the side. Here is a different tuna melt recipe to try.

Tuna Melts
Ingredients:
1 can tuna, drained
1 tablespoon cream cheese
1/4 cup cheddar cheese, shredded
Bread
Directions:
Mix together and place on toasted bread.

Crock pot Roast Chicken

Try adding cubed potatoes, chopped carrots and Brussels sprouts to the crock pot. Season vegetables with salt and pepper and you have a one pot meal.

Ingredients:

4 teaspoon salt

2 teaspoon paprika

1 teaspoon cayenne pepper

1 teaspoon thyme or marjoram

1/2 teaspoon pepper

1 clove garlic, minced

1 large roasting chicken

1 large onion, quartered

Directions:

Mix all the spices including salt, paprika, cayenne pepper, thyme, pepper and garlic, together in a small bowl. Wash the chicken well and pat dry. Place chicken in crock pot and coat the chicken thoroughly with the spice mixture both inside and out. Place the onions in the cavity of chicken. Do not add any liquid. Cover and cook on low 6-8 hours.

Beef Cabbage Soup

Okay, so you are probably thinking cabbage soup no way kids will like this! It is full of vegetables but I tell my kids it's like a treasure hunt because the soup is full of so many different things you get to dig through and find buried treasure. Treasure being the beef or vegetables they really like. There is also a vegetable or two in the soup that kids will avoid but if they are eating most all the rest of the vegetables I let it slide this once.

I made the mistake of adding more than 1/4 Cup rice, I figured I'll just add all the rice I have left in the cupboard. Well it took over the whole soup and didn't work out well. My husband jokingly said it was like Spanish rice. So only put in what it calls for or you can even leave it out and it won't be missed.

Ingredients:
2 pounds ground hamburger, cooked
6-8 cups beef broth
1 -14 1/2-ounce can crushed tomatoes
2 cups potatoes, cubed
1 cup cabbage, shredded
1/2 cup celery, chopped
1/2 cup carrots, sliced
1/2 cup onions, chopped
1/4 cup white rice uncooked or barley
1/2 teaspoon black pepper
1 Tablespoon Worcestershire sauce
1 teaspoon Italian seasoning and 1 teaspoon oregano

Directions:
In crock pot, add cooked hamburger, beef broth and vegetables. Season with salt and pepper, seasonings and Worcestershire sauce. Cook on low 4-6 hours. Add rice and continue to cook several hours.

Chicken Piccata
Ingredients:
1 cup flour or breadcrumbs
1/2 Cup parmesan cheese
1 tablespoon Italian seasoning
1/2 Cup milk
1 lb. chicken breasts
Pasta
2 Tablespoons butter
1/4 Cup honey
juice of one lemon

Directions:
Boil water for pasta. Meanwhile, flatten chicken breasts with kitchen mallet. Then cut chicken into smaller pieces. Mix flour, cheese and seasoning together in flat dish. Pour milk in different flat dish. Place chicken pieces in milk, then coat chicken in flour mixture. Add olive oil to frying pan and brown chicken. Cook pasta. Once chicken is browned. Add in the saucepan, butter, honey and juice of one lemon. Heat several minutes and serve over cooked drained pasta.

Minestrone Soup Recipe
Ingredients:

1 lb. hamburger

1 onion, grated or chopped

3 cloves garlic, minced

2 stalks celery, chopped

2 carrots, diced

small bag frozen corn

small bag frozen green beans

28 oz. can chopped tomatoes

1 can tomato paste

3-4 potatoes, peeled and diced

1/2 head cabbage, chopped

1 teaspoon basil

1/2 teaspoon pepper

2 teaspoons salt

1/2 teaspoon oregano

2 bay leaves

4 cups beef broth or equivalent water and beef bouillon

8 cups water

Directions:

In stock pan, sauté hamburger, onion and garlic. Drain grease and add back to pan. Add remaining ingredients. Stir together and simmer for 30 minutes. This recipe freezes well, also.

Beef Barley Soup

Ingredients:
1-pound ground beef
1 onion chopped or pureed in blender
2 teaspoons oregano
1 large can of tomatoes, pureed in blender
4 Cups beef broth
2/3 Cup barley, uncooked

Directions:
Brown beef with onion. Season with salt and pepper and add oregano. Drain meat and add to a soup pan. Add pureed tomatoes, barley, and beef broth to pan. Cook until barley is tender.

If desired add a bag of frozen vegetables 10-15 minutes before serving

Breakfast Egg Casserole Recipe

Ingredients:

shredded potatoes or hash browns potatoes

shredded cheese, as much as you'd like

1 cup chopped ham, bacon, sausage or turkey

6 eggs

1 -1/2 Cups milk

1/4 Cup pureed, diced or shredded vegetables such as zucchini, mushrooms, broccoli or spinach

salt and pepper

Directions:

In a casserole dish, layer potatoes on the bottom of the pan. Sprinkle cheese on top of potatoes. Add breakfast meat on top. I used cooked turkey bacon in the picture above.

Mix eggs, milk and vegetables together in a bowl. Season with salt and pepper. Pour over top of potatoes and bake at 350 degrees about 45 minutes or until center is firm.

~~A slight variation to this recipe is to use bread slices on the bottom of your pan instead of potatoes. Tear your bread into cubes and place on bottom of pan then follow instructions as above.

Monterey Chicken Recipe

Ingredients:

4 boneless chicken breast

1/4 Cup Barbecue sauce

4 slices bacon

1 Cup Monterey jack and cheddar cheese, shredded

Directions:

In a casserole dish place chicken breasts. Brush chicken with barbecue sauce, add cheese and allow to melt. Place a cooked bacon on top.

I've also cooked the chicken on a George Foremon grill and it has turned out even better.

Homemade Tomato Soup

Ingredients:

4 Tablespoons butter

2 Tablespoons olive oil

1 onion, chopped finely or grated

1/4 cup flour

3 Tablespoons tomato paste

28 oz. chicken broth

2 cans -28 oz. can tomatoes

1/2 teaspoon Italian seasoning

salt and pepper

Directions:

In saucepan melt butter and olive oil. Sauté chopped onion. Whisk in flour and tomato paste until a thick roux. Whisk in chicken broth.

Add tomatoes and seasoning. Turn to low and simmer 20-30 minutes. Puree soup. Serve warm.

~I love this recipe with grilled cheese sandwiches!

Pasta Fagioli Soup

This Pasta Fagioli Soup recipe is a great meal loaded with healthy vegetables. You see this type of soup served often in Italian restaurants.

Ingredients:

1 Tablespoon olive oil
1 lb. ground beef
1 onion, grated or diced
2 carrots, diced
30 oz. can chopped tomatoes
15 oz. can kidney beans, drained and rinsed (this helps cut back on salt)
3 Cups cooked white beans
7-8 Cups beef broth or 7-8 cups water with 6-7 beef bouillon cubes
1 Tablespoon oregano
2 teaspoons pepper
large jar of spaghetti sauce
1 1/2-2 Cups small pasta shapes

Directions:

In large soup pot, add oil, onion and beef. Sauté until beef is browned. Drain excess oil out of pan. Add carrots, tomatoes, beans, beef broth, oregano, spaghetti sauce and pepper. Simmer 5-10 minutes then add in pasta. Continue to simmer until pasta is tender and vegetables are done. Serve with breadsticks.

Corn Chowder Soup

For this chicken corn chowder recipe, I use leftover chicken from a roast chicken. However, you can also use chicken breasts cut into cubes. This makes a great lunch too.

Ingredients:

1 Tablespoon oil
1 onion, grated or chopped small
2 potatoes, peeled and cut in cubes
2 Tablespoons flour
1 chicken bouillon cube
1 1/2 Cup milk
1 1/2 Cup water
1 can corn, drained
1-2 cups chicken, cooked, shredded or cut in cubes
pepper

Directions:

In a soup pan, sauté onion in the oil. Then add potatoes. Sauté several minutes until potatoes brown. In a measuring cup add flour, bouillon and milk. Blend together. Stir into potato mixture. Add water, chicken and corn. Stir together. Season with pepper, as desired. Cook about 10 minutes until thickens and potatoes are tender.

Recipe for Chicken Pot Pie

Here is a great recipe for chicken pot pie. You can change this recipe up by making one large pie or try individual pot pies. Don't buy the frozen pot pies that are high in fat and preservatives. All you need to do is use this recipe and prepare them in mini tin foil pie plates or small ramekins, if you're lucky enough to have some.

You can also cut back on calories by cutting out the bottom pie crust. Fill your pie ingredients on the bottom then add your crust on the top. Don't forget to add slits or use a mini cookie cutter to cut out a shape for the top crust.

Ingredients:
pie dough homemade or store bought
can cream of chicken soup or homemade sauce below
frozen mixed vegetables
2-3 cups shredded chicken
2 tablespoons butter, melted

Directions:
Sprinkle the table with flour and roll out a ball of pie dough into a small circle. Place dough into a pie pan. Roll out the second ball of dough into a circle for the top crust, set aside.

Add vegetables, chicken, and cream soup or homemade sauce to a mixing bowl. Spoon mixture into pie shell. With the second circle use mini cookie cutters or cut slits in the circle. Top pie with second pie crust.

Cut off the excess dough around the edges and pinch the edges together. With a pastry brush, brush tops of pie with melted butter before cooking. Bake at 375 degrees for 30 minutes or until crust is golden brown.

Homemade chicken pot pie sauce to replace cream of chicken soup, if desired, personally we like it a lot better than cream soup!

Ingredients:
1/3 cup butter or stick margarine
1/3 cup all-purpose flour
1/4 teaspoon pepper
1 3/4 cups chicken broth
2/3 cup milk

Directions:
In saucepan melt butter. Whisk in flour until thickens. Whisk in chicken broth and pepper. Bring to a boil until thickens. Whisk in milk and again bring to a boil until thickens set aside and allow to cool.

Easy Homemade Chicken Noodle Soup

Ingredients:
Roast chicken or chicken pieces
1-2 carrots, cut in half
1 onion
1-2 celery ribs with leaves
2 bay leaves

Directions:
Peel and cut ends off of carrots. Cut into 3 pieces. Cut celery ribs in half. Cut onion in quarters.

In a large soup pot, add roast chicken, carrots, a quartered onion, 1-2 celery leaves and bay leaves. Cover with water and bring to a boil. Cook and simmer on medium-low for 1 hour. Drain broth and reserve. Allow chicken to cool slightly and shred. Add another carrot, diced and whatever vegetables you'd like to the broth. Stir in egg noodles and simmer until vegetables and noodles are tender.

Quick Chicken Noodle Soup

Ingredients:
6-8 Cups Chicken broth
1-2 Cups shredded or chopped, cooked chicken
1 Cup chopped carrots, 1 Cup chopped potatoes, 1 Cup chopped celery or substitute one bag of mixed vegetables for fresh vegetables
egg noodles
Add all ingredients to a soup pot and simmer until tender.

Homemade Macaroni and Cheese

Ingredients:

12 oz. Pasta or macaroni
3 Tablespoons butter
3 Tablespoons flour
1 ½ teaspoon mustard
¼ teaspoon salt
2 Cups Evaporated milk
¾ teaspoon Tabasco sauce
2 Cup Cheddar cheese, shredded
1 Cup Gouda cheese shredded
¾ Cup Parmesan cheese

Directions:

Cook pasta. Meanwhile, melt butter in saucepan. Stir in flour, mustard and salt. Cook, whisking constantly. Mixture will thicken. Whisk in milk and Tabasco until mixture is smooth. Cook, until slightly thickened. Stir in 1 ½ Cup cheddar, gouda and parmesan cheese until smooth and melted. Stir in hot pasta. Stir to combine. Spoon mixture into baking dish. Sprinkle with remaining cheddar cheese. Broil until lightly browned. Serve immediately.

Waffle Night

Make it a waffle night with homemade whole wheat waffles, fresh fruit, whip cream, jam or/and bacon or ham on the side. I often puree 2 small zucchini in the blender and add it to the waffle batter.

Whole Wheat Waffles
Ingredients:
2 eggs
2 cups whole wheat flour
1 3/4 cups milk
1/2 cup oil or applesauce
4 teaspoons baking powder
pinch of salt

Directions:
Heat waffle iron. Add all ingredients in mixing bowl. When waffle iron is heated add a scoop of batter into waffle iron and cook until brown. Serve with peanut butter, maple syrup or fresh fruit.

Potato Bar

Kids especially like making their own meals personal so any chance they can fix their dinner however they would like they seem to enjoy the meal more. This potato night we had a simple broccoli and cheese soup and chili to top our potatoes. Some people at our house just prefer their potato plain with a little salt and pepper, too.

Other potato topping ideas could be:
Chopped broccoli
Chopped onions
Cooked bacon pieces
Butter
Sour cream
Ranch dressing
Nacho cheese

Here is our recipe for a simple **Broccoli and Cheese Soup** for topping your potato

Ingredients:
1 Cup milk
1/3 Cup cheese, shredded
1 Cup chopped broccoli
1 Cup chicken broth

Directions:
Cook your broccoli in the chicken broth until broccoli is tender. Stir in milk and cheese and stir until cheese melts. Pour over baked potatoes or eat as is.

Corn Dog Recipes

We've included two corn dog recipes on this page. One is a traditional fried version and the other is a mix between a hot dog roll up and a corn dog which is baked in the oven.

Ingredients:

3/4 Cup cornmeal

3/4 Cup flour

1 teaspoon baking powder

1/4 teaspoon salt

1 egg, beaten

2/3 Cup milk

8 wooden sticks

8 hot dogs

Oil for deep fat frying

Directions:

Using a tall measuring cup or glass will make it easier to dip your hot dog into the mixture and coat the hot dog. If it is easier you can mix it in a bowl and then pour the batter into a tall container. You can also cut your hot dogs in half and it will be easier to coat the whole hot dog and you will easily have a mini corn dog recipe.

Combine cornmeal, flour and egg. Blend together until mixed well. Slowly stir in milk until your batter thickens. Let stand a few minutes while you heat up the oil in a frying pan or deep fat fryer. Heat oil to 375 degrees.
Dip hot dog in batter coating all sides some batter may drip down that is okay too. Fry until golden brown. Drain on a paper towel.

~Any leftover batter can be fried for eating, these are called hush puppies.

Mini Corn Dog Rollup Recipe

Ingredients:

1 3/4 Cup cornmeal

3 1/4 Cups flour

2 teaspoons baking powder

1/2 teaspoon salt

1 Cup sugar

2 Tablespoons butter, soft

1 egg

1 Cup milk

Directions:

In a mixing bowl, blend cornmeal, flour, baking powder, salt and sugar together. Blend in butter, egg and milk and mix well until your batter forms a ball of dough.

Take a piece of your dough and roll into long ropes. Cut 8 hot dogs in half and set all but one aside. Slowly roll hot dog into the rope as shown.

Continue with remaining hot dogs and place each on a cookie sheet. Bake in a 400-degree oven for 10-15 minutes or until dough is lightly browned.

Meatballs

It is super easy and cheaper than buying frozen meatballs to make your own. Using a meatloaf recipe, yes meatloaf recipe, you can create several meals worth of meatballs.

Ingredients:

2 eggs
1 Cup milk
1/2 cup dry bread crumbs
3 teaspoon seasoning salt
1 Tablespoon Worcestershire sauce
1/2 teaspoon pepper
2 lb. ground hamburger

Directions:

Place all ingredients together in bowl and using your hands, combine. Roll small pieces into balls and place on a cookie sheet.

You can thread meatballs on skewers and baked them in the oven for 15-20 minutes at 350 degrees. Make sure you flip over the meatballs half way. You can also brush them with Barbecue Sauce before cooking and again when you flip them over. Or just use sauce for dipping.

Other meatball recipes could be meatball soup or sweet and sour meatballs.

Alfredo Pizza

Prepare the recipe below for Alfredo sauce.

Spread sauce over your pizza crust, sprinkle with mozzarella cheese, then top with chopped cooked chicken and cooked chopped broccoli.

Bake.

Homemade Alfredo Sauce

Ingredients:
2 Tablespoons butter
2 Tablespoons flour
3 Cups milk
1 teaspoon salt
½ teaspoon pepper
Pinch of nutmeg
¾ Cup parmesan cheese

Directions:
To make sauce, melt 2 Tablespoons butter in pan. Add 2 Tablespoons flour, cook, stirring constantly, 1 minute. Whisk in 3 cups milk, 1 teaspoon salt, 1/2 teaspoon ground pepper and a pinch of nutmeg. Bring to a boil. Reduce and simmer several minutes. Stir in 3/4 Cup parmesan cheese.

Chicken Cordon Bleu

Ingredients:
6 chicken breasts
6 slices Swiss cheese or other sliced cheese you like
6 slices ham
can cream chicken soup
½ pint sour cream

Directions:
Beat chicken breast flat with meat tenderizer or rolling pin. Place slices of ham and cheese on top of chicken breast. Place chicken in casserole dish. Stir cream soup and sour cream together. Pour sauce over chicken.

Bake at 400 degrees for 35-40 minutes, or until chicken is done. Allow to cool and freeze chicken breasts in tin foil. When ready to cook, unwrap chicken breast and place in casserole dish. Bake 15-20 minutes. You can also serve with noodles or rice.

~You can also leave the cream soup sauce out and just top with another slice of cheese.

Chicken Broccoli Roll ups

Ingredients:

4 chicken breasts halves
2 slices cheese
1 Cup chopped broccoli
1 Tablespoon flour
½ Cup milk
1 Tablespoon chicken broth
1 teaspoon fresh parsley
¼ teaspoon salt
1/8 teaspoon pepper

Directions:

Flatten chicken by placing chicken bre_____between two sheets of waxed paper. Then pound flat with a kitchen mallet or rolling pin. Cut one cheese slice into four strips. Place one strip in center of each chicken.

Top with chopped broccoli. Roll chicken up and secure with toothpicks if needed. Place in casserole dish. Cook at 350 degrees until no longer pink.

While chicken is cooking, whisk flour and milk together in a saucepan on medium to low heat. When mixture thickens and starts to boil, add broth, parsley, salt and pepper. Whisk together. Add remaining cheese slice and continue cooking until cheese melts. Pour over chicken. Cook another 10 minutes or until heated through.

...ade to order by getting all the add ins ready. Have ...d ins and cook an omelet for each family member

...d ins:
...ed cheese
...d ham
...hopped mushrooms
Chopped onions
Chopped broccoli
Chopped, cooked spinach
diced tomatoes

Directions:
Using a small frying pan, spray with cooking spray and heat on medium heat. In a small bowl, crack 2 eggs and beat. Sprinkle with salt and pepper. Pour eggs into hot pan.

Sprinkle top of your eggs with add ins. Let eggs set until edges can be lifted. Lift edges all around your pan. Scoop spatula underneath omelet and flip. Allow to cook on this side several minutes. Serve.

Pierogi

This is typically a Polish dish but you often find Pierogi in Russia and throughout Eastern European cooking. You can create these with whatever filling you choose. Try cooked ground beef or pork, cheese and potatoes, cabbage or fruit fillings. They are similar to a stuffed dumpling.

Ingredients:
3 cups all-purpose flour
2 eggs
1 cup sour cream
1/2 teaspoon salt

Directions:
In a mixer add flour, eggs, sour cream and salt together. Mix together to form a ball of dough. Take out of mixing bowl and knead on a floured surface 5-10 minutes. Let rest for 30 minutes wrapped in plastic wrap. Roll dough out and cut circles out of the dough by using the bottom of a glass or biscuit cutter.

Potato Cheese Filling
1/2 cup mashed potatoes
1 cup cottage cheese
1 onion, minced
1 egg yolk, beaten
1 teaspoon sugar
1/4 teaspoon salt

Directions:
Sauté onion in butter. Mix mashed potatoes, cottage cheese, sautéed onion, egg yolk, sugar and season with salt and pepper. To assemble pierogi, place a spoonful of filling on each circle dough and moisten ends with water. Seal together by pressing with your finger or using the back of a fork. To cook, bring a large pot of water to boil. Add salt to water. Add pierogi's and cook

about 5 minutes. (they will float to the top of the pot). You can fry these with chopped ham and butter. Or serve this Eastern European cooking recipe with sour cream or drizzle with melted butter.

Potato Gnocchi

A great potato gnocchi recipe that is good with a tomato sauce or a yogurt sauce.

Ingredients:

1 Cup mashed potatoes about 1-2 medium potatoes cooked, diced and mashed
2 eggs
1 teaspoon salt
1 Cup cottage or ricotta cheese
1/4 Cup parmesan cheese, grated -1/2 Cup if you are using grated Parmesan cheese in a shaker like Kraft or a generic brand
2 tablespoons butter, softened
3 Cups flour

Directions:

Cook and mash your potatoes. Set aside. In a mixing bowl, add eggs, salt, cheeses and butter. Blend together. Add in mashed potatoes and flour. Blend together until dough forms a ball. Knead gently on a floured counter. If your dough is too dry add a tablespoon of water until it forms a ball and kneads well.

Separate dough into 4 balls. Roll into thick ropes. Cut each rope into ¾ inch-1-inch pieces.

Pour water into a large pot and add salt. Bring to a boil. Place gnocchi pieces into boiling water. When gnocchi rise to the top take them out with a slotted spoon. Sprinkle with Parmesan cheese and serve with pasta sauce. Serve immediately.

Eggs in Spaghetti Sauce

Ingredients:

Eggs

Spaghetti sauce

Shredded cheese

Directions:

Pour 1 cup or less spaghetti sauce into skillet. Let warm over medium heat. Crack eggs into the pan, one egg for each person, into the sauce.

Salt and pepper eggs. Cover pan with lid. Cook several minutes until eggs are set. Before serving sprinkle with Parmesan cheese or cheese of choice.

Panini

What is a Panini? Simply a sandwich pressed in a grill. The sandwich can include any deli type meat, cooked chicken, roast beef, cheese, sliced vegetables or whatever you like.

Try these in the George foreman grill, that is what I use. However, you can also buy a Panini grill or toastmaster. If you don't have any of the above just make your sandwich, add butter to a hot pan and grill both sides.

Other Panini Sandwich Ideas:

Try adding fresh spinach, tomato slices or pepper strips.
Try a pizza Panini by adding spaghetti sauce, shredded cheese and toasting.

Easy Quesadilla Recipes

Quesadillas are a great last-minute meal. A lot of different flavors you can create too.

Directions:

Add filling on top of a tortilla. Top with second tortilla. Toast on a hot griddle or skillet.

Mexican Quesadilla- Try refried beans and cheese. You can also mix in cooked ground beef to your refried beans if you'd like.

Pizza Quesadilla- pizza sauce, shredded cheese, pepperoni slices, whatever you like on your pizza?

Cheese Quesadilla- whatever shredded cheese you'd like, cheddar cheese, Monterey cheese, etc.

Chicken Quesadilla- add shredded cook chicken, shredded cheese, sliced or chopped vegetables

Alfredo Noodles
Ingredients

Fettuccine noodles or any type noodles you choose
1lb. Broccoli, chopped, * optional
Cook noodles and last few minutes add broccoli. Meanwhile make sauce.

Alfredo Sauce Ingredients:
Melt 2 Tablespoons butter in pan.
Add 2 Tablespoons flour, cook, stirring constantly, 1 minute.
Whisk in 3 cups milk
1 teaspoon salt
1/2 teaspoon ground pepper
a pinch of nutmeg
2 cloves garlic, minced

Bring sauce to a boil. Reduce and simmer several minutes. Then stir in 3/4
Cup parmesan cheese.

Stir Fry

To make an easy stir fry recipe you can buy the frozen package of stir fry vegetables and you'll have your vegetables already prepared. However, if you are using fresh vegetables you can prepare these steps in the morning and it will still save you time at dinner.

I like to use carrots, zucchini, mushrooms, peas and peppers. Cut your vegetables in thin strips or dice them. Green peas, of course, are ready to go as is. Add all vegetables to a Ziploc bag or bowl. Place in the fridge. If you are using meat, prepare marinade and pour in baggie. Try using chicken strips, beef strips or pork strips. If you'd like a shrimp stir fry don't marinade ahead of time. Add meat to your marinade and place in fridge.

For dinner place meat in pan with marinade and cook several minutes. Add vegetables. If you are serving rice with your meal start this the same time as the meat. Try using thin spaghetti noodles instead of rice for a Lo Mein meal. After vegetables and meat are done cooking toss with cooked noodles.

Easy Stir Fry Marinade

If you are not using meat for your recipe you will still need this for the stir fry sauce. Prepare ahead and add as much as you'd like when you are cooking the vegetables.

Ingredients:
1/4 Cup soy sauce
1 Tablespoon Worcestershire sauce
1/4 Cup brown sugar
1/4 Cup water
2 teaspoons ginger
1 garlic cloves, minced

Directions:
Mix above ingredients together. Add to your meat and marinade several hours.

Grilled Chicken

Sometimes I forget simple meals are just as good as complex.
Grill chicken or chicken cubes in a skillet or George Foremon and serve with vegetables.

Roasted Broccoli

You cut broccoli into spears and place on a cookie sheet. Drizzle with olive oil and season with salt and pepper. Toss to evenly coat. Cook for 10-15 minutes on 450 degrees. Stir half way through.

*A yummy idea for kids is to create an open face sandwich with grilled chicken.

Mini Barbecue Meatloaf

Ingredients:

1 egg, beaten
1/3 Cup milk
1/3 Cup Barbecue sauce, divided, leave some for the top
½ Cup crushed stuffing
1 Tablespoon onion soup mix
1 ¼ lbs. Ground beef

Directions:

Place ½ cup stuffing mix in a plastic bag and crush with a rolling pin or kitchen mallet. Add meat to a mixing bowl, then add egg, milk, barbecue sauce, crushed stuffing, and onion soup mix.

Stir ingredients together until well combined. Grease loaf pan or mini loaf pans with shortening or cooking spray. Shape meatloaf into the pan. Spread a little barbecue sauce on the top. Bake at 350 degrees for 15-20 minutes and test with a meat thermometer.

**If you have mini loaf pans or mini cake pans they work great for meatloaf also. If you don't have these available use a muffin pan. Kids can mix and mash the meatloaf together.

Breaded Pork Chop Recipe

This breaded pork chop recipe is so yummy and makes super moist pork chops. it will soon be a favorite at your house. I prepare this recipe ahead of time and leave it in the fridge. Then bake before dinner.

Ingredients:
4-6 boneless pork loin chops-I bought thick ones and sliced them in half lengthwise
1/2 cup all-purpose flour
1/2 teaspoon seasoned salt
1/4 Cup milk, plain yogurt or buttermilk
1/2 cup Italian-style dry bread crumbs

Directions:
Set three flat pie plates or flat dishes next to each other. In one add flour and seasoning salt, in another add milk and the last add bread crumbs. Dip pork chops in flour first covering both sides. Then dip both sides in milk. Then dip both sides in bread crumbs. Place in a casserole dish. Spray pork chops with cooking spray. This will make your pork chop crispy without frying it. Bake at 375 degrees for 20-30 minutes or until pork is done.

Chicken Enchilada

This recipe for chicken enchiladas can be changed slightly by substituting white or brown rice for the cooked white beans. You can also leave the beans out if you'd like. This is a great recipe for freezing extra. It also can be prepared the night before or morning and left in the fridge until cooking time.

Ingredients:

4 Cups shredded cooked chicken
8 oz. cream cheese, softened
1/2 Cup salsa
1 cup shredded cheese
1 cup cooked white beans
salt and pepper
1 can of cream of chicken soup
1 cup milk
whole wheat flour tortillas

Directions:

In large bowl, blend chicken, cream cheese, salsa, cheese, beans and salt and pepper. Stir together to combine. In separate bowl, stir cream chicken soup and milk together until blended. Add 1/2 cup of cream of chicken soup to chicken mixture. Blend together.

Add 1/4 cup of chicken, or as much as desired, to a tortilla. Roll up and place in casserole dish. Continue with remaining tortillas and chicken mixture. Pour remaining cream chicken sauce over the top of your tortillas. Bake at 350 degrees for 20 minutes.

Serve with chopped avocado, tomatoes or prepared guacamole. Make an extra one for the freezer!

Chicken Wings

Ingredients:

½ Cup brown sugar
¼ Cup soy sauce
¼ Cup water
1 Tablespoon Worcestershire sauce
1 tsp. lemon juice
1 tsp. ginger
garlic to taste

Directions:

Mix together and marinate chicken for several hours before cooking. To cook place marinated chicken in a 13x9 or larger pan. Cook at 400 degrees for 45 minutes-1 hour or until chicken is tender.

Grilled Hamburgers

Forget getting your hamburger from a drive through. It is so much better homemade and less fat!

Ingredients:
Lean ground beef
Salt and pepper

Directions:
Season hamburger and form into patties. Grill and serve with whole wheat buns.

~If you'd like a little more seasoning add dash of Worcestershire sauce and 1-2 Tablespoons dry onion soup mix.

Chicken Tortilla Soup

Our best chicken tortilla soup recipe. This recipe is great served with tortilla chips, chopped avocado, sour cream and shredded cheese. It also freezes well.

Ingredients:

8 Cups water
1 can chopped tomatoes
1 can corn, drained
1 Tablespoon lime or lemon juice
3-4 chicken breasts
1/4 Cup salsa

Directions:

Add chicken and water to soup pot. Bring to a boil. Then simmer 15-20 minutes until chicken is tender. Cut chicken into small pieces with kitchen scissors. Stir in chopped tomatoes, corn and lemon juice

Homemade Cream of Broccoli Soup

You'll love this homemade cream of broccoli soup recipe. You can puree this soup into a cream soup or forgo the blending and leave it chunky. My kids prefer it chunky whereas I like it creamy so I usually split the recipe in half when it is done and blend half and leave the rest as is for the kids.

Ingredients:
1 Tablespoon olive oil
1 onion, grated
1-2 bunches of fresh broccoli cut or one bag frozen broccoli
4 Cups chicken broth
2 potatoes, cubed
2 Cups milk
1 Cup cheddar cheese, shredded
salt and pepper to taste

Directions:
Heat oil in soup pan and cook onion and potato cubes. Sauté. Season with salt and pepper. Add chicken broth and cook until potatoes are slightly tender. Add broccoli to soup pan. Cook until broccoli and potatoes are tender. Add milk and cheese and stir until cheese is melted. Add to blender and puree into cream soup or use an immersion blender.

Lentil Soup
Ingredients:
2 tablespoons olive oil
1 onion chopped
3 carrots grated or cut in small pieces
¾ teaspoon marjoram
1 28 oz. can tomatoes
7 cups beef or chicken broth
1 ½ cups dried lentils

Directions:
In skillet or large saucepan sauté onions and carrots in 2 tablespoons olive oil until tender. In blender puree tomatoes with their juice and add to saucepan. Add broth, onion mixture and lentils together. Cook on medium-low covered for one hour or until lentils are tender. Season with salt, pepper and parsley if desired. Allow to cool and pour into freezer containers

How to Make Cabbage Rolls

To learn how to make cabbage rolls can be a little time consuming at first. However, once you learn the technique of removing the cabbage leaves they are a great recipe for its hidden vegetable factor.

It takes a little longer to prepare the cabbage leaves so it is great for a weekend meal. It can also be cooked in the crock pot instead of the oven. Now one might get a little scared about the idea of feeding kids cabbage rolls. However, in my recipe I also add chopped cabbage to the hamburger mixture so if kids take out the meat mixture in the cabbage leaf and leave the cabbage behind I'm okay with that. The meat inside the cabbage roll turns out moist and delicious having cooked wrapped in a cabbage leaf.

Ingredients:

large head of cabbage, cored
1 medium onion, quartered
2 big carrots, cut in chunks
1 lb. lean beef, ground, not cooked
1-2 cup white rice or brown rice, cooked
2 bay leaves
2 (8 ounce) cans tomato sauce
tomato juice
sour cream, topping if desired

Directions:

Cut around core of cabbage. Prepare cabbage leaves by boiling head of cabbage several minutes. Remove leaves as they fall off and continue to soften leaves until most are removed. In blender or food processor, puree carrots, 1 onion, 1/2 cup cabbage and 1/2 cup tomato sauce. Pour into a mixing bowl and add 2 lbs. hamburger, uncooked. Add in 1-2 cups cooked rice. Combine all together. Place meat mixture on a cabbage leaf and roll up. Place each cabbage roll in casserole dish. Add bay leaf and tomato juice or more tomato sauce. Cover with extra cabbage leaves. Cook 350 degrees covered with tin foil and bake about 1 hour. Top with sour cream, if desired.

Sweet and Sour Chicken
Ingredients:
4 chicken breasts, cut in cubes
can pineapple chunks (save juice)
one garlic clove, minced
1/4 Cup soy sauce
1 teaspoon ginger
1-2 carrots cut in small pieces
1 green pepper cut in pieces

Directions:
Add all ingredients together in a Ziploc bag. Freeze. When ready to cook. Add to saucepan and allow to simmer 30 minutes or until chicken is cooked through. Cook rice to go with the meal.

~We like to make this same recipe with meatballs in place of chicken.

Gyro Recipe

We use chicken or pork cut in strips for this gyro recipe. It is topped with a cucumber yogurt sauce and served in a flat bread, pita bread or tortilla. Both parts of this recipe need to marinade so it is a great make ahead recipe. All you need to do at dinnertime is cook marinated meat. You can serve with carrot, pepper and cucumbers sticks as the yogurt dressing makes a good vegetable dip.

Cucumber Gyro Sandwich Recipe

Ingredients:
1 lb. pork loin or chicken breasts, cut into cubes or strips
1/4 Cup olive oil
1/4 Cup lemon juice
1 Tablespoons mustard
2 cloves garlic, minced
1 teaspoon dried oregano
dash of salt and pepper
Directions:
Mix oil, lemon juice, mustard, garlic, oregano, salt and pepper together in a bowl or Ziploc baggie. Add meat and marinade several hours.

Yogurt Dressing
Ingredients:
1 Cup plain yogurt
1 cucumber chopped in food processor
½ teaspoon crushed garlic
½ teaspoon dill weed
Directions:
Add ingredients together and chill in refrigerator.
Prepare the marinated meat and yogurt dressing and store in fridge in the morning.

Cheesy Noodle Casserole

This cheesy noodle casserole is creamy and super kid friendly. You can change this recipe by adding ground hamburger to your spaghetti sauce or leaving out the mushrooms. You can also add sliced olives in place of mushrooms.

Ingredients:
1 small bag of spiral pasta or 2 cups
large jar spaghetti sauce
small can mushrooms, optional
1/2 cup plain yogurt or sour cream
6-8 Cheese slices
Mozzarella cheese, shredded for topping

Directions:
Cook pasta noodles, drain and set aside. In a casserole dish, drizzle spaghetti sauce over the bottom of the dish. Add half of the pasta on top of the spaghetti sauce. Add more spaghetti sauce and spread over noodles. Spread sour cream or plain yogurt over the top for the next layer. Top with cheese slices.

Add the rest of your pasta noodles. Then spread remaining spaghetti sauce over the noodles. Sprinkle the top with mozzarella cheese. Bake at 350 degrees for 20-30 minutes just until the spaghetti sauce starts to bubble and the cheese is melted.

Chicken Lo Mein

Serve for dinner and include leftovers in your lunch box.

Ingredients:

8 ounces uncooked linguine noodles
chicken breast halves, cubed
1/2 cup soy sauce
1 tablespoon brown sugar
1 clove garlic, minced
1/4 cup chicken broth
1 (16-ounce) bag frozen stir fry vegetables or whatever vegetables you have on hand

Directions:

Cook noodles. While noodles are cooking, cook chicken pieces in a frying pan. Add soy sauce, brown sugar, garlic and chicken broth. Stir in frozen vegetables and cook covered on medium. When chicken is cooked through and vegetables are tender mix drained noodles into chicken mixture. Serve immediately.

White Bean Soup
Ingredients:
3 Cups white beans, dried
1 onion, quartered
2 bay leaves
1-2 potatoes, cubed
2 carrots, cubed

Directions:
You can add in chopped ham, polish sausages, cooked chicken or ground hamburger if you'd like or leave out.

Cover dried beans with water and let sit overnight. In the morning drain the water and place beans in a pot. Cover with water and add a quartered onion and 2 bay leaves. Allow to cook on medium-low for 1 hour or until beans are slightly tender.

~If using canned beans forgo the directions above and start here.
At dinnertime add potatoes and carrots to the beans. Add more water if needed to cover all the vegetables. Bring to a boil and cook until potatoes are tender.

Chicken Roll Ups
Ingredients:

crescent dough homemade or store bought

3-4 chicken breasts, cooked and chopped

8 oz. cream cheese

salt and pepper

1/4-1/2 Cup shredded cheese

Directions:

In a bowl, blend together cooked chicken, cream cheese and cheese. Sprinkle with salt and pepper. Roll crescent dough out into a circle and cut into triangles or unroll dough if using store bought. Place chicken mixture on the end of each triangle.

Roll fat end of triangle down to pointed end. Place on cookie sheet. Bake at 350 degrees for 10-15 minutes or until dough is golden brown. Serve with cream of mushroom soup, cream of chicken soup or without a sauce.

Chinese Hamburger

This Chinese Hamburger recipe has very few ingredients and can easily be mixed together at dinnertime. If you are looking for a quick meal use instant rice and canned cream of mushroom soup.

Ingredients:
2-3 Cups cooked rice
1/2-1 lb. ground hamburger
1 Tablespoon soy sauce
2-3 Cups cream of mushroom soup or 2 cans

Directions:
Step 1: Make rice.
Step 2: While rice is cooking, brown hamburger. Drain and set aside.
Step 3: Mix cooked rice with browned hamburger.
Step 4: Stir in cream of mushroom soup and soy sauce.
Step 5: Taste test and add more soy sauce if desired.

Homemade Cream of Mushroom Soup

Ingredients:
8 oz. fresh mushrooms, diced or sliced
1 onion, shredded or chopped
1 garlic clove, minced
2 Tablespoons butter

Directions:
In soup pan, melt butter and sauté mushrooms, onion and garlic for several minutes. Whisk in 2 Tablespoons flour. Blend together. Then add in, 2 Cups chicken broth. Allow to cook several minutes. Add 1 Cup milk and whisk together. Season with a dash of pepper. Heat several minutes and use in any recipe that calls for cream of mushroom soup.

tay with Peanut Sauce

ken marinade and place in the fridge in the morning. Then mix
.r peanut sauce and store in fridge as well.

Ingredients:
6-8 drumsticks-but you can use chicken breasts or chicken thighs also
1/4 Cup orange juice
1/4 Cup soy sauce
3 Tablespoons honey
2 garlic cloves, minced
1 Tablespoon ginger

Directions:
In large measuring cup, add orange juice, soy sauce, honey, garlic and
ginger. Blend together and pour into large Ziploc baggie. Add drumsticks
and marinade several hours in the fridge.

Chicken Peanut Satay Sauce
Ingredients:
1/2 Cup chicken broth
1/2 Cup orange juice
1/4 Cup peanut butter

Directions:
Mix three ingredients together and store in a bowl in the fridge until ready to
use.

At dinner time take out chicken drumsticks and place in a casserole safe
dish. Cook for 15 minutes. Pour peanut sauce over the top and continue to
bake 15-20 minutes or until chicken is tender and no longer pink.

Lemon Mustard Chicken
Ingredients:
roast chicken
1/3 Cup olive oil
2 Teaspoons dry mustard
Juice of one lemon
one lemon cut in slices

Directions:
Wash and dry roast chicken. Place in crock pot. In small bowl mix olive oil, mustard and lemon juice. Blend together and pour over roast chicken. Add sliced lemons inside the chicken cavity and around the edges.

Ham and Noodle Casserole

You can change your noodles easily in this recipe by using whatever shape or type you have on hand. Our favorite is using frozen tortellini.

Ingredients:
bag of frozen tortellini
bag of frozen broccoli
white sauce, recipe below
ham cubes

Directions:
Boil water and add frozen tortellini and broccoli. Cook until both are tender. Meanwhile make a basic white sauce. Drain noodles and broccoli. Place inside casserole dish or back into drained pot. Add chopped ham. Pour white sauce over the top. Stir to combine. Serve immediately.

White Sauce
Ingredients:
1 Tablespoon butter
1 Tablespoon flour
1 Cup milk
salt and pepper to taste
1 teaspoon other seasonings, such as garlic or Italian seasoning if desired

Directions:
Melt butter. Whisk in flour making a roux. Whisk in milk and seasonings. Simmer until thickens.

Tuna Casserole

Ingredients:

8 oz. noodles of choice-we like seashells or fettuccine noodles

1 can healthy request cream mushroom soup

1/2 cup plain yogurt

2 Tablespoons-4 oz. cream cheese

2 cans tuna or less if you desire

1 small pkg. frozen peas

Pepper

Directions:

Cook noodles, drain and place in baking dish. Sprinkle top of noodles with peas. The hot noodles will unthaw the peas quickly, but you can add the peas several minutes before the noodles are done cooking and drain peas and noodles together.

In mixing bowl, add cream of mushroom soup, yogurt, cream cheese and tuna. Stir until well blended. Season with pepper and stir into noodles. Serve immediately.

Lumpias

Lumpias are like eggrolls. They are a dish that comes from the Philippines.

Ingredients:
Lumpia wrappers
Cooked ground beef
2-3 carrots, shredded

Directions:
Mix cooked beef and carrots together in bowl. Season with salt and pepper. Heat a small pan of oil on the stove to deep fat fry. Or you can bake this in the oven.
Place 1-2 tablespoons of beef mixture on end of a lumpia wrapper. Roll up and tuck in sides. Continue to roll to the end. Fry in oil until crispy.
Serve with teriyaki sauce or other dipping sauce.

**Another simple filling idea is cooked shredded chicken seasoned with 1-2 tablespoons soy sauce and a sprinkle of ginger. (Or to taste.)

Crepes

Ingredients:
3 eggs
1 ¼ Cup milk
¾ Cup flour
1 Tablespoons sugar
½ tsp. Salt

Directions:

Whisk ingredients together. Ladle about 1/4 Cup or so of batter in a hot frying pan. Flip to other side when edges will lift. These are great rolled and served with berries on top. You can serve these like a breakfast for dinner or roll ham and cheese or chicken salad in your crepe. Better yet have a variety of fillings for the family to choose their own.

Beef Brisket
Ingredients:
1 onion
Carrots cut in chunks as many as desired
Potatoes cut in chunks as many as desired
1 Cup beef broth
1 teaspoon Worcestershire sauce
One whole clove of garlic
Bay leaf
Cabbage cut in wedges

Directions:
Place cut vegetables on bottom of crock pot. Place corned beef brisket on the top. In mixing bowl combine broth and Worcestershire sauce. Pour over top of brisket. Add garlic clove and bay leaf. Cook on low 6-8 hours. Add cabbage to top of pot half way through cooking time.

Spaghetti Jambalaya

Ingredients:

1 pkg. sweet sausage, cut in chunks

3 chicken breasts, cut in chunks

2 garlic cloves

salt and pepper

1 teaspoon Italian seasoning

Directions:

In large skillet sauté all ingredients above until browned. Take out of pan and set aside.

Add 1/2-1 pkg. of spaghetti noodles that have been broken in 2-inch pieces to your skillet. Stir fry noodles until lightly brown. Add 1 can tomato sauce, 2 bay leaves and 2 Cups water. Water should just cover noodles. Add your meat back to pan and simmer for 10 minutes or until noodles are tender and water has evaporated.

Shepherd's Pie

You can change this recipe easily by using ground hamburger, beef cubes, lamb, or even ground turkey. You can also choose your family's favorite vegetables. If you'd like to use fresh vegetables chop and boil for 5-7 minutes before stirring in. This will help your vegetables to come out not so crunchy! Our family's favorite vegetable in this easy shepherd's pie is fresh or frozen green beans but you can try mixed vegetables, corn or carrots and pea mix.

Ingredients:
1 lb. ground beef or beef cubes
1 onion, grated or chopped
1 carrot, grated or diced
1 garlic, minced
1 teaspoon Italian seasoning
salt and pepper
1/4 Cup beef broth
1 teaspoon Worcestershire sauce
1 Tablespoon tomato paste
1 Tablespoon dry onion soup mix
small bag of frozen vegetables- such as green beans or peas and carrot mix
mashed potatoes
cheddar cheese

Directions:
In a skillet brown your beef with onion, carrot and garlic. Season with Italian seasoning and salt and pepper. Add in beef broth, Worcestershire sauce, tomato paste and onion soup mix and stir until blended. Stir in vegetables and pour into a sprayed pie plate or casserole dish. Top with mashed potatoes and spread over the top. Sprinkle with cheddar cheese and bake at 350 degrees for 30-40 minutes.

Kabobs

For dinner marinate chicken or steak cubes (see the recipes below) and create your kabob with meat, mushrooms, peppers, tomatoes or other vegetables.

Meat Kabob Marinade

Ingredients:
1/3 Cup Worcestershire sauce
1/3 Cup soy sauce
1/3 Cup water
1/3 Cup ketchup
1/4 teaspoon ginger
1 garlic clove, minced
2 Tablespoons brown sugar

Directions:
Add ingredients together in jar and shake until combined. This marinade is enough for about 1-2 pound of meat or vegetables. Marinade meat for several hours and grill or bake.

You can also marinade vegetables in this such as mushrooms, broccoli, carrots or cauliflower for 1-2 hours.

Quick and Simple Meat Marinade

Try a balsamic vinaigrette either homemade or store bought. Pour 1/2 Cup in a ziploc baggie and place chicken or beef cubes in bag. Marinade several hours. Grill or bake.

Herbed Baked Fish

Ingredients:
1/2 Cup herb stuffing mix, crushed very fine
2 Tablespoons margarine, melted
4 frozen fish portions
2 teaspoons lemon juice

Directions:
Adjust the oven to 425 and allow it to preheat.

Spray a rectangular baking dish well with a non-stick cooking spray.

Place the stuffing mix into a bowl.

Add the melted margarine and toss to coat the stuffing well.

Lay the fish into the prepared baking dish.

Drizzle the lemon juice evenly over the fish.

Spread the stuffing mix over the top.

Bake for 18 minutes or until the fish flakes easily with a fork.

Any type of frozen fish will work in this recipe. If you have a favorite stuffing mix other than herb try it to see how it tastes. You may also add a little grated Parmesan cheese to the stuffing mix before adding the melted butter.

Fajitas

Kids can easily help with this recipe by stirring the marinade ingredients together and pouring into a baggie with the meat. Cut chicken or beef into strips and marinade in a plastic Ziploc baggie overnight or prepare in the morning.

Marinade ingredients:

2 tablespoons lime juice
3 tablespoons olive oil
2 teaspoons chili powder
1 garlic clove, minced
1 1/2 teaspoon seasoning salt
1 1/2 teaspoon oregano

Directions:

Cut 2 green, yellow, red or a combination of peppers into slices. Cut 1 onion into rings. Cut 1-2 carrots into sticks. To prepare, cook marinade meat including the juice, pepper slices, carrot sticks and sliced onions in a pan for about 10 minutes until meat is cooked through. Serve on flour tortillas with sour cream or guacamole.

Made in the USA
Middletown, DE
12 September 2019